AF269864

KENDRICK LAMAR and TUPAC SHAKUR

Influential Rappers

Tom Jackson

Lerner Publications ◆ Minneapolis

Content consultant credit: Dr. Aminah Pilgrim, Berklee College of Music; Boston, Massachusetts

Lerner Publications Company
An imprint of Lerner Publishing Group, Inc.
241 First Avenue North
Minneapolis, MN 55401 USA

For reading levels and more information, look up this title at www.lernerbooks.com.

Main body text set in Eurostile LT Pro.
Typeface provided by Linotype.

Library of Congress Cataloging-in-Publication Data

Names: Jackson, Tom, 1972-author.
Title: Kendrick Lamar and Tupac Shakur : influential rappers / Tom Jackson.
Description: Minneapolis : Lerner Publications, 2024. | Series: Musicians and their inspirations | Includes bibliographical references and index. | Audience: Ages 8-12 | Audience: Grades 4-6 | Summary: "Kendrick Lamar draws influences from many areas in his life when it comes to music, but his biggest inspiration is Tupac Shakur. Young readers learn more about their music, lives, influence, and more"—Provided by publisher.
Identifiers: LCCN 2023048890 (print) | LCCN 2023048891 (ebook) | ISBN 9798765626696 (library binding) | ISBN 9798765629109 (paperback) | ISBN 9798765635728 (epub)
Subjects: LCSH: Lamar, Kendrick, 1987-–Juvenile literature. | Shakur, Tupac, 1971-1996–Juvenile literature. | Rap musicians–United States–Biography–Juvenile literature. | LCGFT: Biographies.
Classification: LCC ML3930.L136 J33 2024 (print) | LCC ML3930.L136 (ebook) | DDC 782.421649092/2 [B]–dc23/eng/20231017

LC record available at https://lccn.loc.gov/2023048890
LC ebook record available at https://lccn.loc.gov/2023048891

Manufactured in the United States of America

1 - CG - 7/15/24

TABLE OF CONTENTS

Introduction

Lamar was set on a course for stardom after seeing his inspiration Shakur.

Kendrick Lamar says that Tupac Shakur changed his life. When Lamar was around eight years old, Shakur paid a visit to his neighborhood in Compton, California. The older musician was with another hip-hop star, Dr. Dre. The pair were filming a music video in the area. Lamar's father had been in the same area. When he found out the two rappers were filming, he got his son. They were in the crowd watching the two legends drive by in a white car.

Kendrick Lamar never spoke to Shakur. Shakur died the following year. About twenty years later, Lamar wrote his hero a letter. He talked about his joy and excitement at seeing Shakur. He talked about becoming inspired by him. "The people that you touched on that small intersection changed lives forever," Lamar said. "I told myself I wanted to be a voice for man one day."

Over fifty years after the birth of hip-hop, Shakur remains an influential rapper. He inspired Lamar and the next generation of world-class hip-hop artists.

Shakur was one of the most famous rappers of his generation.

The Early Days

Both Lamar and Shakur grew up in tough neighborhoods. They transformed their childhood experiences into music.

Shakur's birth name was Lesane Parish Crooks. When he was one year old, his mother changed it to Tupac. She was a member of the Black Panther Party, a political group in the 1960s–1980s that wanted positive change for African Americans. At the time, many people were wary of the Black Panther Party, including the US government. Shakur's mother chose to rename him after a political hero from Peru. The name Tupac symbolized greatness and someone who tried to create change.

Shakur spent most of his childhood moving from place to place. He later went to the Baltimore School of the Arts in Maryland. There, he wrote poetry and studied acting, dance, and music.

Shakur was born in 1971 in Brooklyn, New York.

Shakur (right)
with his mother,
Afeni (left)

On the West Coast

When he was seventeen, Shakur moved to Marin City, California. His family had a hard time paying the bills. His mother also had a drug addiction. An addiction happens when a person thinks they need something to live, even when it might be bad for them. The stress from these things influenced Shakur to get involved in gangs, where he sold illegal drugs. His experiences with both later found their way into his lyrics.

Shakur began recording tracks in 1989 under the name MC New York. Later after changing his stage name to 2Pac, Shakur released his first solo album, *2Pacalypse Now*, in 1992. It was his breakout album.

INSPIRING THE INSPIRATION

HIP-HOP

Shakur was greatly influenced by politics growing up, partly due to his mother's connection to the Black Panther Party. He found inspiration in the political lyrics of earlier hip-hop acts such as Public Enemy and Ice Cube. Shakur was also inspired by the work of the English playwright William Shakespeare. He said, "[Shakespeare] wrote some of the rawest stories, man."

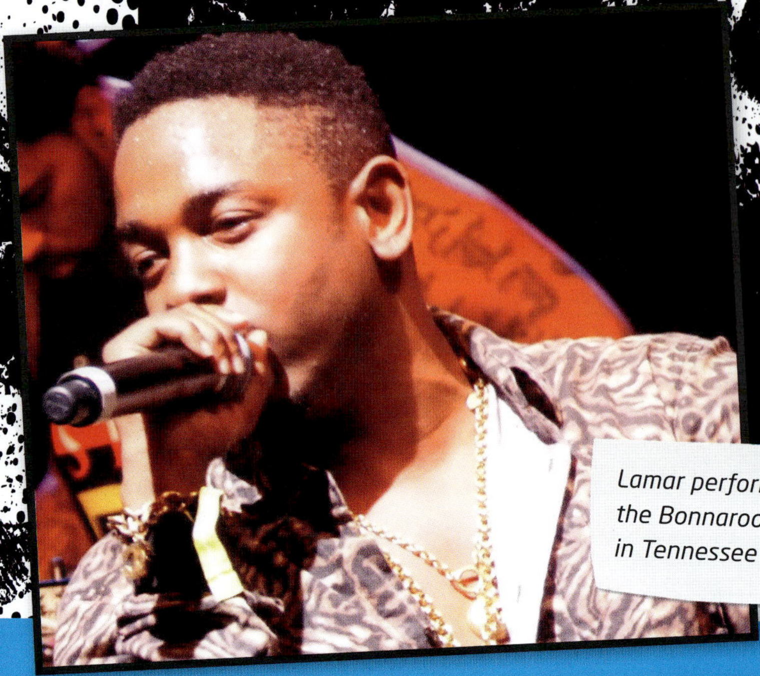

Lamar performing at the Bonnaroo Festival in Tennessee in 2012

Starting Young

Kendrick Lamar Duckworth grew up in Compton, California. The area had a high crime rate. His family relied on government assistance (welfare payments) to get by. Lamar turned to music early on.

Lamar became interested in hip-hop and rap music at a young age. He began writing his own lyrics. Lamar released a mixtape under the name K. Dot when he was sixteen. The mixtape was so impressive a record label signed Lamar as an artist.

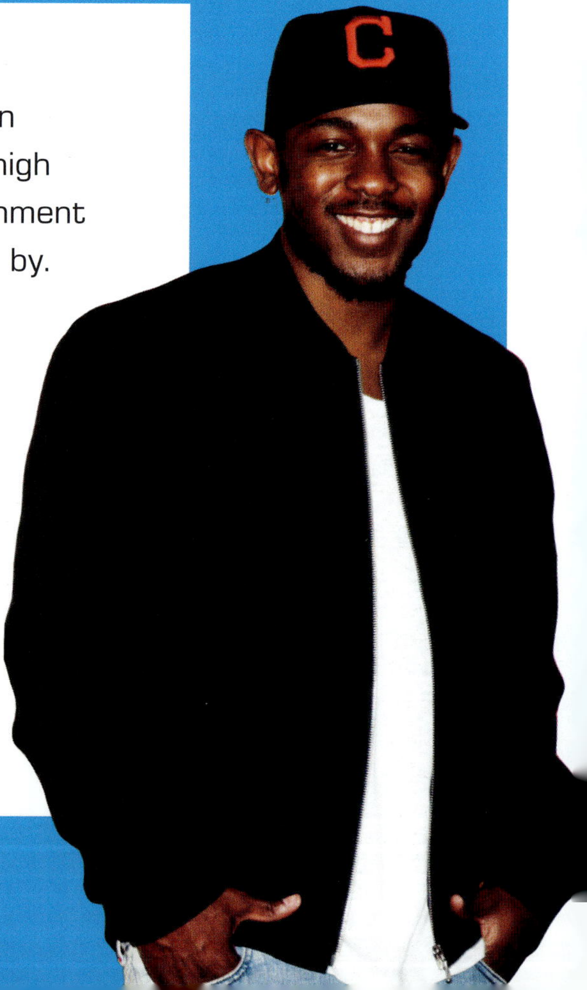

Dr. Dre was both Shakur's friend and a mentor to Lamar.

Lamar released more mixtapes as K. Dot. Then in 2010, he put out the album *Overly Dedicated* under the name Kendrick Lamar.

Lamar grew in popularity. He performed on other hip-hop artists' tracks. In 2011, he released his album *Section.80*. Lamar signed with Dr. Dre's record label a year later. In 2012, Lamar released his album *good kid, m.A.A.D. City*, which featured several hit tracks. Like Shakur before him, Lamar's music drew from his experiences.

CHAPTER 2

Finding Flow

Lamar and Shakur used music to share their thoughts. They approached songwriting in different ways, but they put in the same hours to make something great.

Shakur wrote his music quickly. He did not limit himself in how he made music. He often got into a flow and improvised rap lyrics over a beat. He didn't stop when he made mistakes. Instead, he just kept on going. This let him be more creative. He often recorded songs for hours at a time.

The following day, Shakur would come back to the studio. He fixed his mistakes and filled in the gaps left in tracks recorded the day before. He found this way of working enjoyable. It let him keep having ideas without having to stop and restart.

Shakur (left) on the set of a film in 1993 with Janet Jackson (right)

Shakur performing with Digital Underground in 1991

Shakur's lyrics often were about wider social issues, including gang culture, racism, and police brutality. His first rap was about gun control. He wrote it at school after a friend from Baltimore was shot while playing with a gun. Shakur wanted change in the world. He used his lyrics as a way to talk about it. "I got a big mouth," he said. "I can't help it. I talk from my heart. I'm real."

Keeping Notes

Lamar's writing process is different. Writing takes him longer than Shakur. Each track takes many months to come together. He keeps notes of things that inspire him, from meeting new people to visiting different places. These notes help remind him of how he felt at that moment even months later.

Lamar performing in Austin, Texas, in 2016

In the studio, he finds a sound that reminds him of those feelings. Then he creates his lyrics. He writes about many personal themes, including mental health challenges.

Lamar performs in Las Vegas, Nevada, during the Life Is Beautiful Festival in 2015.

Lamar on stage at a festival in Spain in 2016

Shakur and Lamar both used samples in their songs. A sample is a pre-existing recording by someone else that is excerpted and put into a song to create something new. A sample can be a rhythm, melody, or speech. Lamar once sampled Shakur's voice in one of his songs.

Like Shakur did before him, Lamar works for many hours in the studio. In the past, he used to think about the listener and what they wanted to hear. Since then, he's focused on being honest with himself. "At the end of the day, you're going to know [that my music] comes from a real place," he said. "I'm unapologetic, I'm not compromising, and it's going to feel me."

CHAPTER 3

Street Style

Hip-hop is about more than just music. It's also about style. One of the main elements of the genre is fashion.

Shakur performed around fifty live shows in his career. He often appeared on stage with a band, dancers, and backup singers. Shakur could usually be seen wearing a twisted bandana around his shaved head. This became a signature look for him. Sometimes he took off his top and performed wearing only a large golden crucifix around his neck. Many rappers copied this look after Shakur's death.

Lamar has appeared in hundreds of shows. In 2022, he went on his Big Steppers world tour. He visited six different continents and saw millions of fans. But it's not just his music that has attracted attention from fans. They also love his fashion.

Shakur's clothing choices helped later guide hip-hop fashion.

Bandanas were one of Shakur's signature looks.

Lamar's stage performances have elaborate lighting and many backup dancers.

Designer Clothes

Lamar tends to wear baggy clothing. On and off the stage, fans can see him wear designer-brand clothing, such as Louis Vuitton and more. On one of his tours, Lamar wore a crown of thorns. It was a nod to Jesus Christ. Christ wore a crown of woven twigs on the cross. Lamar's crown was silver and made by the jewelers Tiffany and Co.

More Than Music

During his 2022 tour, Lamar turned the stage into an opera set. He played a character called Mr. Morale after his album, *Mr. Morale and the Big Steppers*. A large cast of dancers took the stage. English actor Helen Mirren even recorded the narration to help tell the story of Mr. Morale's treatment for mental health. The show has been described as a hip-hop opera.

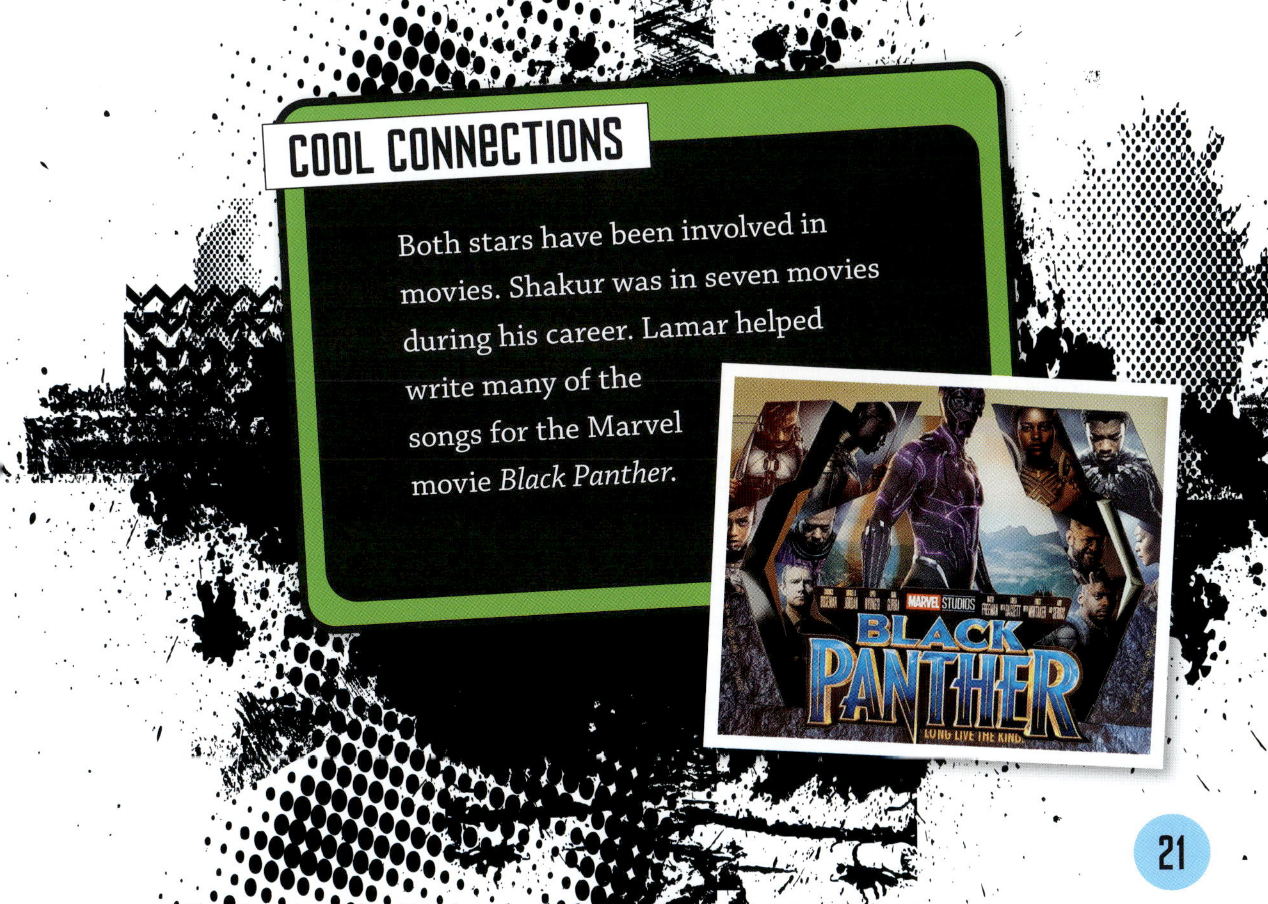

COOL CONNECTIONS

Both stars have been involved in movies. Shakur was in seven movies during his career. Lamar helped write many of the songs for the Marvel movie *Black Panther*.

Global Superstars

With their lyrics and messages, Lamar and Shakur reach listeners of many generations, including past, present, and future lovers of hip-hop.

In 1996, Shakur was shot by a gunman while driving with friends through Las Vegas, Nevada. A few days later, he died of his injuries in the hospital.

Shakur was already a big star in music and movies, but after his death, his impact on hip-hop has had a lasting effect. Stars such as Eminem, J. Cole, Drake, and more have said he was a big influence on them. In 2002, Shakur was inducted into the Hip-Hop Hall of Fame.

An exhibit from the Tupac Shakur Museum in Los Angeles, California

Shakur arriving at the world premiere of one of his movies in 1996

Shakur's family celebrate his star being added to the Hollywood Walk of Fame in 2023.

In 2010, the US Library of Congress added Shakur's song "Dear Mama" to the National Recording Registry. This was only the third rap song to be included. In 2017, Shakur was added to the Rock and Roll Hall of Fame. A few years later, Shakur got his own star added to the Hollywood Walk of Fame.

COOL CONNECTIONS

In 2023, *Billboard* magazine ranked Shakur as the fourth-best rapper of all time. Lamar is number two.

Great Success

Lamar is one of the most highly awarded rap stars in history. He's won seventeen Grammy Awards. Six of them are for Best Rap Performance. Lamar holds the record for most BET Hip Hop Awards, having won twenty-five awards. In 2018, Lamar won the Pulitzer Prize for Music for his fourth studio album. This was the first time this award had been given to an artist who did not produce classical music or jazz.

Lamar celebrates winning at the MTV Video Music Awards in 2017.

From an early age, Lamar was inspired by the honesty in Shakur's music. Both artists helped change and grow hip-hop. Besides becoming a global genre, hip-hop also found its way into other media, such as books, film, and TV. Although the artists followed different paths, both became influential figures in the world of music.

Lamar performing in Rotterdam, Netherlands, in 2023

Your Inspiration

Both Lamar and Shakur grew up in tough neighborhoods, but both became global superstars. Just because Lamar and Shakur made it big doesn't mean they forgot their roots though. Lamar donates his money to many charities, including programs for the Compton Unified School District in California, the place where he grew up. After Shakur's death, his mother founded the Tupac Amaru Shakur Foundation. The foundation provides resources for those who have experienced trauma, as well as promotes awareness for mental health.

Who inspires you? They don't have to be someone famous. It could be anyone: your best friend, your teacher, your aunt, or a person in your community. Why do they inspire you? What can you learn from them?

IMPORTANT DATES

1989	Tupac Shakur starts performing as MC New York.
1992	Shakur releases his first solo album, *2Pacalypse Now*.
1996	Shakur is killed by a gunman in Las Vegas.
2003	Kendrick Lamar releases his first mixtape under the name K. Dot.
2011	Lamar releases the album *Section.80* under the name Kendrick Lamar.
2012	Lamar signs with Dr. Dre's record label.
2017	Shakur is added to the Rock and Roll Hall of Fame.
2018	Lamar is the first hip-hop artist to win the Pulitzer Prize for Music for his fourth studio album.
2022	Lamar goes on his Big Steppers world tour.
2023	Shakur gets his own star on the Hollywood Walk of Fame.

GLOSSARY

crucifix: a cross-shaped object

improvise: to make up or arrange something without planning it in advance

mixtape: an album of songs usually recorded and given out without the help of a record company

playwright: a person who writes plays

police brutality: excessive and unwarranted use of force by police

political: to do with governments

racism: discrimination based on race

social issue: a problem that affects many people living in a society

studio album: a set of original songs by an artist recorded in a studio and sold by a record company

welfare payment: money given by the government to people who do not have enough money to buy food and other important things

SOURCE NOTES

5   Joe Taysom, "The Moment Tupac Shakur Inspired Kendrick Lamar to Become a Rapper," Hip Hop Hero, Updated January 23, 2022, https://hiphophero.com/tupac-shakur-inspired-kendrick-lamar-be-a-rapper/.

9   L-FRESH the LION, and Rosa Gollan, "Tupac Was One of the Greatest Rappers of All Time and Here's Why," ABC News, Updated October 5, 2020, https://www.abc.net.au/news/2017-09-06/tupac-was-one-of-the-greatest-rappers-of-all-time-heres-why/8870400.

14   Jessica Sager, "62 Tupac Shakur Quotes To Inspire You To Make Positive Changes and Remind You to Never Surrender," *Parade*, September 24, 2023, https://parade.com/1237476/jessicasager/tupac-quotes/.

17   Drew Morisey, "Kendrick Lamar Teaches How to Start Writing a Rap," Rap Game Now, Updated January 13, 2022, https://rapgamenow.com/how-to-start-writing-a-rap-kendrick/.

Learn More

Britannica Kids: Kendrick Lamar
https://kids.britannica.com/students/article/Kendrick-Lamar/631144

Britannica Kids: Tupac Shakur
https://kids.britannica.com/students/article/Tupac-Shakur/604099

Elizabeth, Jordannah. *A Child's Introduction to Hip Hop: The Beats, Rhymes, and Roots of a Musical Revolution*. New York: Black Dog & Leventhal, 2023.

Kiddle: Kendrick Lamar Facts for Kids
https://kids.kiddle.co/Kendrick_Lamar

Kiddle: Tupac Shakur Facts for Kids
https://kids.kiddle.co/Tupac_Shakur

Markovics, Joyce L. *Kendrick Lamar*. Ann Arbor, MI: Cherry Lake Publishing, 2023.

Schwartz, Heather E. *Kendrick Lamar: Platinum Rap Artist*. Minneapolis: Lerner Publications, 2024.

Shea, Therese M. *Kendrick Lamar: Becoming the Voice of Compton*. New York: Enslow Publishing, 2020.

INDEX

PHOTO ACKNOWLEDGMENTS

Image credits: fuzheado/Wikimedia Commons, p. 4; DMI/The LIFE Picture Collection/Shutterstock, p. 5; Mtv/Amaru/Paramount/Kobal/Shutterstock, p. 7a; Baltimore Sun/Wikimedia Commons, p. 7b; Leonard Zhukovsky/Shutterstock.com, p. 7c; Mtv/Amaru/Paramount/Kobal/Shutterstock, p. 8; Skyhawk/Shutterstock.com, p. 9a; Gyvafoto/Shutterstock.com, p. 9b; Andrei Moldovan/Dreamstime.com, p. 9c; John Elbas/flickr.com/Wikimedia Commons, p. 10a; Kathy Hutchins/Shutterstock.com, p. 10b Featureflash/Dreamstime.com, p. 11; PeopleImages.com - Yuri A/Shutterstock.com, p. 13a; Moviestore/Shutterstock, p. 13b; Pat Johnson/Shutterstock, p. 14; Taylor Creek Media/Dreamstime.com, p. 15; Koby Dagan/Shutterstock.com, p. 16a; Christian Bertrand/Shutterstock.com, p. 16b; Mtvfilms/Amaruentertainment/Paramountpictures/Kobal/Shutterstock, p. 19a; Startraks/Shutterstock, p. 19b; kennyysun/flickr.com/Wikimedia Commons, p. 20a; Maja Smiejkowska/Shutterstock, p. 20b; Faiz Zaki/Shutterstock.com, p. 21; Jim Ruymen/UPI/Shutterstock, p. 23a; Bei/Shutterstock, p. 23b; Jim Ruymen/UPI/Shutterstock, p. 24; Feature Flash Photo Agency/Shutterstock.com, p. 25; Hollandse Hoogte/Shutterstock, p. 26. Cover: Hutchinsphoto/Dreamstime.com; CelebrityArcheology.com/Alamy Stock Photo.